Book 1:
The Best of Beautiful Netherlands For Tourists
BY GETAWAY GUIDES

&

Book 2:
Dutch for Beginners
BY GETAWAY GUIDES

Book 1:

The Best Of Beautiful Netherlands for Tourists

BY GETAWAY GUIDES

The Ultimate Guide for Netherlands Top Sites, Restaurants, Shopping, and Beaches for Tourists!

Table Of Contents

Introduction

I want to thank you and congratulate you for purchasing the book, "The Best Of Beautiful Netherlands for Tourists: The Ultimate Guide for Netherlands Top Sites, Restaurants, Shopping, and Beaches for Tourists!".

This book contains proven steps and strategies on how to enjoy a vacation in The Netherlands.

The Netherlands is known across the world as a progressive country. Many tourists go to this country for different reasons. This book shares information about the various tourist destinations, shopping sites, restaurants, and beaches in different parts of this country. A chapter is also dedicated to the arts and culture of The Netherlands so that tourists will understand what kind of country they will be visiting.

Thanks again for purchasing this book, I hope you enjoy it!

Chapter 1: Tourism in The Netherlands

The Netherlands has always been a haven for tourists from around the world. In fact, there is a yearly increase in the number of tourists who visit the country. World renowned for its Delft pottery, windmills, and tulips, the Netherlands is also famous for its free-spirited capital, Amsterdam. Found in the northwestern part of Europe, the small country boasts of the Frisian Islands, canals and bridges, farmlands, beautiful villages, and highly populated cities.

Amsterdam is the most popular city in the country because of the party scene, red light district, the Anne Frank House, art museums, medieval architecture, and scenic canals. Tourists can start from this city and take advantage of different day tours to check out different places around the country. The Hague is known as the Dutch royal family's home as well as the seat of government. Zaanse Schans and Volendam are popular for their customs, windmills, costumes, and traditional Dutch houses. The town of Lisse is a popular tourist spot during spring for its flowers. The town of Alkmaar is a great place to visit for its cheese market.

The Netherlands is known for its cuisine which basically consists of vegetables and meat, Dutch apple pie, smoked sausage, and fried meatballs. Tourists can also opt to dine in different international restaurants around the country. In terms of transportation needs, tourists can go around by buses and trains. Because of the good roads and flat land, they can also go cycling.

For tourists going to The Netherlands, they have to ensure that their passports have enough unused pages and are valid for at least 3 months after departure from the country. Tourists may require securing a visa before traveling to the country. However, US citizens are not required to have a visa if they only plan to stay in the country for a maximum of 3 months.

Chapter 2: Tourism in Various Regions of the Netherlands

In 2011, tourists flocked to the northern part of The Netherlands. An estimated 6 million guests visited the region. The southern part, on the other hand, had 1.4 million tourists. Belgians, Britons, and Germans were the top visitors of The Netherlands. The country is famous for its 7 World Heritage Sites. Because it is a small country, tourists can travel from north to south in just one hour.

North Holland

Amsterdam is located in the northern part of the country. Around 4.3 million foreigners visited the city in 2011. Famous museums like Rijkmuseum, Ann Frank House, and the Van Gogh Museum are top tourist spots. The city's canal ring is considered a World Heritage Site. Drug tourists flock to Amsterdam because cannabis consumption and prostitution are legal in The Netherlands. On the northern part of the capital, tourists visit the Zaanse Schans for its windmills, and Marken and Volendam for their old fishing villages. Alkmaar is famous for its old center and cheese market. The castle of Muideeslot is found on the southeast side of Amsterdam. The town of Naarden has a well preserved star fort while Haarlem is noted for its old city center and historical legacy. Zandvoort, a seaside resort near Haarlem is famous for its car racing circuit.

South Holland

In 2013, around 849,000 tourists visited the Keukenhof, which is noted as the largest flower garden in the world. Keukenhof is only open to the public during the spring season. Kinderdijk is famous for its 19 windmills and is recognized as a World Heritage Site. On the other hand, The Hague is often visited for its government buildings like the Ridderzaal and the Binnenhof. The Mauritshuis is an art museum which is also frequented by tourists in the area. Tourists troop to Scheveningen because of its beach. A miniature park is found in Madurodam.

Found in the northern part of The Hague, Leiden is popular for its national museums like the Rijkmuseum van Oudheden and Naturalis. Considered as the world's oldest botanical garden, the Hortud Botanicus Leiden is also a popular tourist site. Katwijk and Noordwijk are popular resorts by the sea. Delft is located on the southern part of The Hague and is popular for its old center and pottery. William the Silent, touted as the founder of modern Netherlands, has a museum in his name in Delft.

Other Regions In The Netherlands

The city of Utrecht has the tallest church tower in the country. It also houses the Netherlands Railway Museum and the Musical Clock Museum. Tourists can also visit the Slot Zuylen Castle and the Kasteel de Haar. Efteling is near Kaatsheuvel and is considered one of the oldest theme park around the world. It is also the country's entertainment park. Effenaar is famous as a music venue in Eindhoven. The Slot Loevenstein is a castle located in the province of Gelderland. The country's oldest city, Nijmegen, is popular because of the International Four Day March during the month of

July. Another popular site in Gelderland is the Netherlands Open Air Museum. Mudflat hiking is possible from Friesland mainland to the West Frisian Islands during low tide. Middleburg boasts of various seaside resorts in the province of Zeeland.

Chapter 3: Top Tourist Sites In The Netherlands

Some parts of The Netherlands are reclaimed from the sea. Most tourists only visit Amsterdam. However, the country still has a lot to offer aside from its capital city. Cycling is perfect in most areas because the landscape is flat and crisscrossed with canals. Guests can visit historic town centers and other tourist sites around The Netherlands. The long coastline is peppered with sandy beaches and protective dunes. Flower gardens are popular during springtime.

The Delta Project is a series of storm surge barriers, dikes, locks, sluices, and dams which were built from 1950 to 1997 in South Holland and Zeeland. The American Society of Civil Engineers included the site to the Seven Wonders of the Modern World. Maastricht Vrijthof is a popular city square in South Holland. It showcases the Saint Jan's Cathedral and Saint Servatius Church. Huge festivals are also held in the city of Maastricht all year round.

Found in Amsterdam, the Rijksmuseum is the coubtry's most prestigious and largest art and history museum. Works of Rembrandt and Vermeer are showcased there. Kinderdijk, on the other hand, has the most number of Dutch windmills in one site. The Hoge Veluwe National Park is the biggest continuous nature reserve with woodlands, sand dunes, and heath lands. Inside the park is the Kroller-Muller Museum which has a huge collection of Vincent van Gogh's paintings.

To promote the country's flower industry, The Netherlands has Keukenhog Gardens which is recognized as the largest flower garden in the world. Yearly, about 7 million flower bulbs like tulips, daffodils, and hyacinths are planted in the park. The garden is open from late March up to the middle of May. The Delft City Hall is a tourist attraction because of its Renaissance building. Designed by Hendrick de Keyser, it has undergone a lot of changes and was restored to its original Renaissance appearance in the 20th century.

The West Frisian Islands is a series of islands found in the North Sea. Licensed guides help the guests tour the islands by walking on mudflat. Known as Rembrandt's birthplace, Leiden boasts of beautiful canals. Popular for its oldest university, its old center is the 2nd largest 17th-century town center in the country. Finally, Amsterdam's canals form concentric belts which consist of 3 major canals like Keizersgracht, Prinsengracht, and Herengracht.

Gouda is popular among day trippers. It is famous for its cheese, clay pipes, candles, and syrup waffles. Tourists can take the highway and railway to go to this city. Rotterdam, on the other hand, is considered the most modern city in The Netherlands. Tourists go to this city for its carnivals and festivals during the summer season. The Museum Boijmans Van Beuningen has a collection of works of masters like Rembrandt, Bosch, Van Gogh, and Dali. The university city of Groningen has 2 colleges. Its Groninger Museum is the most modern and innovative in the country.

Unofficially dubbed as the flower city, Haarlem hosts the Annual Bloemencorso Parade. Located near the Spaarne River, it has medieval structures which tourists can experience. Museums and architecture are stunning and shopping is always enjoyable in Haarlem. The Teylers Museum is the country's oldest museum and features science, arts, and natural history exhibits. Utrecht, on the other hand, has a rich Middle Age history. The University of Utrecht is the largest university in the country. The Gothic Cathedral of Saint Martin, the Museum Speelklok, the Rietveld Schroder House, and the Dom Tower are also popular tourist spots.

The city of Maastricht is famous for its Vestigingswerkens, Saint Jan's Cathedral, and Saint Servatius Church. Furthermore, Helpoort and St. Pietersberg Caves are also worth visiting. Popular for its Royal Picture Gallery Mauritshuis and the Gemeentemuseum Den Haag, The Hague offers a glimpse of Dutch Royalty. Tourists enjoy the North Sea during the warm months in Scheveningen. They can enjoy the international art galleries, cozy shops, and luxury stores. The Hague is home to the seat of government, known as the Binnenhof. Madurodam is the city's miniature city.

The city of Delft is progressive. Tourists can enjoy a day trip to visit the Prinsenhof, a museum which showcases a lot of intriguing works. Leiden, a beautiful city, is a popular tourist spot because of its tree-lined, scenic canals as well as its lush parks, wooden bridges, and old windmills. Visitors can enjoy a boat ride along its canals. Lastly, Amsterdam is famous for its unique coffee shops, pubs, galleries, and shops. Its popular museums are favorites among museum hoppers.

Chapter 4: Top Restaurants In The Netherlands

The Dutch cuisine is a sophisticated mix of exotic and local ingredients using traditional French culinary techniques. Some restaurants use Zeeland lamb, pigeon, local livestock, langoustine, lobsters, and mussels.

Located near the southwest part of The Netherlands, near the Belgian border, Oud Sluis is a restaurant and guesthouse in the town of Sluis and famous for its various oyster preparations. It also offers home-grown and seasonal produce. Restaurant De Librije is inside a library of a 15th-century monastery with old world charm and high ceilings. It offers tasting menus with exotic and classic ingredients. Cod stomach, rabbit kidneys, acid bomb, and -20 degrees Celsius-cooked egg yolk.

Ron Gastrobar is in Amsterdam and offers an eclectic menu in surprising textures and tastes. Ciel Bleu is famous for its cuisine as well as the view it offers to Amsterdam diners. The menu includes truffled macaroni, lobster in farmhouse butter, Siberian sturgeon caviar, and King crab. De Lindenhof, on the other hand, is a restaurant in a farmhouse with lush garden. It offers Belgian and Dutch cuisine. It is located in a village known as the "Venice of the Netherlands", Giethoorn. It can only be accessed through boats because cars are not allowed in the village.

Located at the north of Haarkem, De Bokkedoorns is a French restaurant offering pigeon in red beet sauce, cod sashimi with creme fraiche, and blini. 't Brouwerskolkje is also in Haarlem and offers a menu using a blend of molecular and traditional techniques. Because it only has 6 tables, tourists must make reservations. Boreas has a great garden terrace and modern ambiance in a 20th-century villa in Heeze. Its menu is a mix of innovation and tradition.

Located near the coast of Zeeland and the beautiful villages of Zierikzee, Veere, Middleburg, and Yerseke, Inter Scaldes is both a manor and a restaurant. The menu includes Zeeland lamb, bass, mussels, lobster, and oyster. Da Vinci is in Maasbracht and offers simple menu which changes every 5 weeks. Restaurant Beluga offers impeccable service. The menu is rich in local seasonal ingredients. The restaurant is located in Plein.

Parkheuvel is located in Rotterdam and is popular for its seafood. Da Zwethheul, on the other hand, is famous for its tartar of scallops, goose liver and truffle, and jelly of lobster. The restaurant is near the Schie River in Schipluiden. Just outside of Maastricht, in a small village, is De Leuf. The restaurant is known for 4 and 6 course menus. Guests can stay overnight in this picturesque farm. Finally, De Leest is famous for its wine and seafood. It is situated outside of Apeldorn.

Chapter 5: Top Shopping Sites In The Netherlands

Shopping In Amsterdam

The capital city of Amsterdam has a lot to offer to tourist shoppers. The area of Amsterdam-Zuid is a haven for tourists who prefer luxury brands. From Leidseplein to P.C. Hooftstraat, visitors can find the most luxurious and exclusive shops. For those tourists who prefer exclusive and original boutiques, the 9 Straatjes is the perfect shopping place. These small streets of fashion boutiques are located between the Singel, Prinsengracht, Leidsestraat, and Rozengracht.

Aside from restaurants, architecture, and museums, Amsterdam has a lot of fashion talent. The city center offers huge shopping streets such as Nieuwendijk, Kalverstraat, and Leidsestraat. World-renowned fashion chains and other shops are to be found in the city center. Smaller designer shops are in Jordaan. Chic shopping streets like Beethovenstraat, Van Baerlestraat, and PC Hooftstraat which offer international brands are in Zuid. The district of De Wallen has Oudezijds Achterburgwal offers various special designer shops.

Shopping In Rotterdam

A lot of unique shops are found in Rotterdam. Tourists, who want to buy something ordinary, will be surprised at what the city can offer. Groos is a concept store which sells Rotterdam-made products only while ANSH caters to women who prefer exclusive brands. Tourists who prefer talented yet new designers can check out Nen. Men and women can surely find affordable vintage and timeless pieces. Women who love to shop for shoes will surely find shopping at Betsy Palmer a delightful experience.

C. Cruden is a store which sells special denim products while Ginza sells exclusive sneakers. Tourists who want to shop for accessories, tutus, coats, trench coats, and sweatshirts can buy exclusive brands at Objet Trouve. They can find exclusive but affordable items at Louen. Those tourists who enjoy a Rock 'n Roll lifestyle will surely finf something retro at Very Cherry. A concept store like Gussie & Doortje sells great food, art, interior items, and vintage apparel. The street of Beurstraverse has big stores which sell popular brands while the districts of Pannekoekstraat & Nieuwemarkt offer special design, retro, and Bohemian shops.

The street of Witte de Withstraat offers avant-garde fashion boutiques, cafes, and galleries. For the young and trendy, the district of De Meent has single-brand shops and concept stores. For shoes, jewelry, and fashion shops, tourists can also head to the Nieuwe Binnenweg and Oude Binnenweg. The fashion district of Rotterdam can be found in Kruiskade and Van Oldebarneveltstraat. Lastly, the district of Oude Noorden is full of creative business people and young designers.

Shopping In The Hague

The city center of The Hague offers popular brands in the streets of Grote Marktstraat, Haagse Bluf, and Spuistraat. Sophisticated brands are found in Frederiksstraat, Denneweg, and Plaats square. Exclusive shoe boutiques and haute couture are in Molenstraat and Hoogstraat. The street of Frederik Hendriklaan has everything for each shopper. It offers food, home decors, gifts, and fashion items. Tourists who prefer unique items troop to this street.

Shopping In Maastricht

A lot of markets are found in the city of Maastricht. Tourists can find a lot fresh food, antique furniture, and other wares. Near the city hall and the mansions, visitors can check out the Maastricht Market which is open on Wednesdays and Fridays only. Fresh produce, food, cosmetics, clothes, flowers, and plants are sold in various stalls. On Wednesdays, there are about 200 stalls offering various products to consumers. On Fridays, additional stalls are opened for the fish market. The Stationsstraat, on the other hand, sells organic products on Thursdays. On Saturdays, it is transformed into a flea market.

Shopping In Utrecht

The city of Utrecht is a perfect place for shopping. The city center's Lijnmarkt has fashion and shoe stores. The Oude Gracht, on the other hand, offers different jewelry and special fashion shops. The shopping streets of Domstraat and Korte Jansstraat are popular to tourists who prefer specialty shops. Visitors who want to shop in exclusive, small boutiques can head to the historical streets of Korte Minrebroederstraat and Schoutenstraat.

Like the city of Maastricht, Utrecht also has markets. In fact, the city center hosts 3 large markets. The fabric market is found in Breedstraat, which is recognized as the oldest and largest fabric market in the Netherlands. it is open on Saturdays until 1pm. The flower market is open every Saturday in Janskerkhof and in the streets of Bakkerbrug and Oude Gracht. Lastly, the general market is open every Wednesday, Friday, and Saturday at Vredenburg.

Chapter 6: Top Beaches in The Netherlands

Aside from charming windmills and beautiful landscapes, The Netherlands is also famous for its beaches. Each year, a lot of tourists visit the beaches to enjoy the sea and the sand. The beaches of Zeeland, Flevoland, South Holland, North Holland, Groningen, and Friesland are top tourist attractions during the summer.

The beach of Zandvoort is found in the northern part of the country. Frequented by tourists, it is a nudist beach with a lot of restaurants, bars, and nature reserves. Visitors can enjoy kitesurfing, sailing, and windsurfing. The beach resort in Scheveningen is touted to be the country's best beach resort. It has a beautiful lighthouse, a harbor, an esplanade, and a pier. Guests can enjoy windsurfing. The beach also boasts of different restaurants, cafes, and bars.

Another popular beach for the family is Egmond aan Zee which also showcases a small museum and a fishing village. Tourists can find horses and wild foxes in the nearby dunes. The beach in Texel is frequented by adventurous and active visitors. Guests enjoy the mud walk and a bicycle ride around the area. The dune landscape also features a natural reserve.

Nudist Beaches In The Netherlands

Tourists become curious about the many naturist beaches in the country. Most of them haven't experienced going to a nudist beach because it is prohibited in their country of origin. In the Netherlands, nudism is permitted. Nudists have separate beaches or may have a part of the beach reserved for their use. The nudist beach in Callantsoog is considered the first nudist beach in the country. It was established in 1973? Nude sunbathers also have their own area on the beach. This beach can be accessed by train from Amsterdam. Tourists can take Intercity train to Schagen then take the Conexxion bus 152 to Callantsoog. They have to walk for 20 minutes to get to the beach.

Zandvoort beach has a place dedicated for nudists. It also offers drinks, meals, and snacks to them. Clothed patrons can have the other pavilions not assigned to nudists. Tourists can take train at Amsterdam CS if they want to go Zandvoort. They can get off at Zandvoort aan Zee then ride the Connexxion bus 81 to the beach. After alighting from the bus, they have to walk about 20 minutes to reach their destination. The beaches of Bloemendaal and Velsen share a nudist beach. Tourists can check out the other attractions surrounding the nudist area. This beach can be reached by taking the train at the Amsterdam Sloterdijk station. Travelers can then take the Connexxion Regioline 82 bus which will take them to IJmuiden aan Zee.

There's also a nudist beach at the northern part of The Netherlands. It is between Purmerend and Zaandam, near the Stootersplas lake. The Baaiegatstrand has been improved and was made safer and more spacious. This nudist beach can be accessed by taking the Amsterdam CS train. Tourists then ride the bus 92 to De Kunstgreep and walk for 25 minutes to the beach. Lastly, nudists try nude relaxation, recreation, and sports at Flevo Natuur. It is not really a beach but nudists can ride horses, fish, surf, sail, swim, and sunbathe near Lake Nijkerkernauw in the Hulkesteinse forest. Tourists go to Flevo Natuur by taking the the Intercity train at Amsterdam CS to Almere Centrum. They take the Connexxion bus 160 to the Wielseweg bus stop the on walk for 15 minutes to the park.

Beach Hopping in The Netherlands

The coast of The Netherlands stretches from the Wadden Sea Islands to Zeeland. Beach bars, family beaches, surfer hangouts, and narurist areas have their own places in the region. The water can be cold and brown unlike the crystal clear blue and warm waters of the Mediterranean. Temperatures can range from 2 degrees Celsius to 20 degrees Celsius. Surf schools recommend using a wetsuit in order to deal with the cold waters. The beach waters are analyzed regularly by the infrastructure ministry during the summer season to check the water quality.

If the beach has a blue flag, it means that it is safe and clean. Not all beaches in the country has a blue flag because some beaches have sewage problems. Each year, millions of visitors go the Dutch beaches. German tourists are the top visitors. Guests can explore the flora and fauna, bike to the dunes, try out the local cuisine, and take yoga, beach football, and surf lessons. A total of 350 summer pavilions are prepared to welcome tourists during the summer season.

Travelers who take a Dutch beach holiday can opt for bed & breakfat, campsite, holiday park, or a hotel experience. Beach huts are also available in warmer months. During the winter season, tourists can kite surf, jog, or walk around the beach.

Chapter 7: Arts and Culture in The Netherlands

The Netherlands is a densely-populated, small country which is located in Western Europe. It is adjacent to Germany, Belgium, and the North Sea. The cities of Rotterdam, The Hague, and Amsterdam are the most important and largest cities. The country name means Low Country because of its flat and low geography. It is the primary exporter of agriculture and food products to the United States of America. The country is governed as a constitutional monarchy and parliamentary democracy. It is regarded as a liberal nation which legalized euthanasia, prostitution, and abortion. Its drug policy is considered as progressive. Same-sex marriage was legalizes in 2001.

In the world of arts, The Netherlands has world-renowned painters like Jacob van Ruysdael, Jan Steen, Johannes Vermeer, and Rembrandt van Rijn in the 17th century. From the 19th to the 20th century, it has produced painters like Piet Mondriaan and Vincent van Gogh. Spinoza and Erasmus are popular philosophers. During its Golden Age, the country has produced famous writers like P.C. Hooft and Joosr van den Vondel. In the 29th century, The Netherlands had writers like Willem Frederik Hermans, Gerard Reve, Cees Nooteboom, Hella S. Haasse, Simon Vestdijk, Jan Wolkers, and Harry Mulisch. The Diary of Anne Frank has been translated to different languages. Dutch building replicas are found in Nagasaki, Japan and Shenyang, China. Tourists visit The Netherlands because of its cannabis, Delftware pottery, cheese, wooden shoes, tulips, and windmills.

Social behavior is dictated by the Dutch etiquette code. Books have been written about the Dutch etiquette. Some of these customs are still practiced in some Dutch regions. Furthermore, European etiquette is also practiced in the country. The Dutch people are modern, individualistic, and egalitarian. They see themselves as self-reliant, independent, and modest. Ability is valued over dependency. The Dutch don't like non-essential things. In fact, ostentatious behavior is frowned upon. Spending a lot of money in public is a show-off and is even considered a vice.

A luxurious lifestyle is considered a waste of money. The Dutch people are proud of their international involvement in various affairs. They are proud of their rich art history and cultural heritage. In terms of manners, they are blunt, informal, and have a no-nonsense attitude. They also follow basic behaviors. Other cultures consider the Dutch as patronizing and impersonal. Some people even consider them rude. Their cuisine is shape by farming ang fishing practices. By tradition, their cuisine is straightforward and simple with little meat and a lot of vegetables. Bread with toppings is considered breakfast and lunch while meat, potatoes, and vegetables are served at dinner. Their diet is rich in fat and carbohydrates which reflect the needs of laborers in the country. In the 20th century, this diet became more modern. Most Dutch cities now offer international cuisines.

Music traditions are aplenty in The Netherlands. Traditional music consists of simple rhythm and melody with straightforward refrains and couplets. Songs are often about loneliness, death, and love. Traditional musical instruments include the barrel organ and accordion. Andre Hazes, Frans Bauer, and Jan Smith are known as traditional musicians. Modern pop and rock music started in the 1960s and were influenced by music from the USA and Britain. Dutch bands like Focus, Golden Earring, and Shocking Blue enjoyed monumental success not only in the country but in international fronts as well. By the 1980s, songs were written in the Dutch language. Currently, pop music enjoys air waves in both languages. Symphonic Metal bands Within Temptation and Epica with pop/jazz singer Caro Emerald are enjoying international success.

Many Dutch films enjoyed international recognition and distribution. The Fourth Man, Spetters, Soldier of Orange, and Turkish Delight were some of the internationally known films of director Paul Verhoeven. He also directed Hollywood movies like Basic Instinct and RoboCop. In 2006, he went back to directing Dutch films through Black Book. Fons Rademakers, Dick Maas, and Jan de Bont also became world-renowned Dutch film directors. Dutch actors like Derek de Lint, Jeroen Krabbe, Rutger Hauer, Carice van Houten, and Famke Janssen became successful internationally.

The world of sports has a huge following in The Netherlands. About 25% of the whole population is registered in various sports clubs. About 2/3 of the population has weekly sports activities. Football is very popular in the country, along with volleyball and field hockey. In terms of individual sports, golf, gymnastics, and tennis are very popular. The Netherlands has won a total of 266 medals from the Summer Olympics and 110 medals from the Winter Olympics. The women's hockey team is very successful in the World Cup while the country's baseball team has lorded over the European championship by winning 20 of the 32 games at stake. During the 2014 Winter Olympics, the speed skaters from The Netherlands have won 23 out of the 36 medals. Motorcycle racing is also popular in the country. The TT Assen Circuit has hosted the yearly Motorcycle World Championship since 1949.

The Netherlands is a country rich in culture and the arts. It's not surprising to find out that tourists flock to the country to experience first-hand what this European country has to offer. Aside from its rich culture, the country has a lot of tourist attractions, shopping and restaurant locations, as well as beautiful beaches for everyone. Tourists from around the world will surely find their The Netherlands experience truly a marvelous and enjoyable experience of a lifetime.

Conclusion

Thank you again for purchasing this book!

I hope this book was able to help you to understand the culture and the arts in The Netherlands as well as inspire you take that well-deserved vacation to this country.

The next step is to book that flight to The Netherlands!

Finally, if you enjoyed this book, please take the time to share your thoughts and post a review on Amazon. We do our best to reach out to readers and provide the best value we can. Your positive review will help us achieve that. It'd be greatly appreciated!

Thank you and good luck!

Book 2:

Dutch for Beginners
BY GETAWAY GUIDES

The Best Handbook for Learning to Speak Dutch!

Table Of Contents

Introduction

I want to thank you and congratulate you for purchasing the book, *"Dutch for Beginners: The Best Handbook for Learning to Speak Dutch!"*

This book contains proven steps and strategies on how to learn the Dutch language for beginners.

Some people are intimidated by the Dutch language because they think that it is a hard to learn. Although it is harder than other languages such as Spanish or English, Dutch is still easier to learn than many languages especially those that have their own unique characters such as Arabic, Chinese, Japanese and Russian. It is still considered one of the easiest languages to learn by native and non-native English speakers.

It is important for you to know some practical tips and information that will make it easier for you to learn the Dutch language. This book will provide you with some useful tips and information about learning the Dutch language that will be useful for beginners like you.

Thanks again for purchasing this book, I hope you enjoy it!

Chapter 1: The Benefits of Learning How to Speak Dutch

When learning any foreign language, it is important that you know the benefits that you will get to keep you motivated. So why should you learn how to speak Dutch if you can already speak English or other foreign languages? Here are the benefits of learning how to speak Dutch.

It is widely spoken in Europe

About sixteen million people in Denmark and six million more in Flanders speak the Dutch language. It is also widely spoken in different countries and regions in Europe. In fact, it is considered as the sixth widely spoken language in the continent. This alone makes Dutch an important language to learn.

If you are planning to visit or live in The Netherlands, Belgium or other European regions where Dutch is the official language, you will be able to communicate more easily with the natives. Your travels will also be more enjoyable because learning the language of a country is the first step to understanding its rich culture, history and traditions. You will be able to understand public signs and ask directions from people without any trouble if you know how to speak their language.

It can be useful for work

If you work for a multinational company, your ability to speak Dutch may be useful in case you need to communicate with a Dutch client or colleague. It will give you an edge over your coworkers because you are the only one who knows how to speak the language. If your company needs to send someone to The Netherlands or Belgium to participate in a seminar or conference, you will surely be chosen by your boss because you are the only one who can speak the language. Being able to speak a foreign language will open a lot of doors for you if you are working in a multinational company that has clients and colleagues all over the world.

It makes studying in a European country easier

If you are going to study in The Netherlands, Belgium or other European countries, knowing how to speak Dutch will be extremely useful for you. In fact, you will have a bigger chance at getting accepted in European schools if you already know how to speak their language. It will be easier for you to communicate with your host family (if you have one), your classmates and your teachers.

It helps you enrich your roots

If one of your parents or grandparents is Dutch or if both of your parents are Dutch but you were born in the USA, learning how to speak the language will help you get in touch with your roots. This will also make attending reunions so much easier especially if most of your relatives speak Dutch. You can also visit relatives in The Netherlands or Belgium or wherever your roots came from and staying with them for a short vacation wouldn't be too hard.

It helps you understand the world better

By learning a second language, you become more open-minded about the world you live in and the different cultures of different countries. If you know how to speak Dutch, you will be able to watch Dutch films, listen to Dutch music, read Dutch literature and appreciate Dutch art and pop culture. This increases your understanding of how the world works and that there is still a lot more to see outside the country you live in.

It gives you a sense of achievement

Being able to speak a foreign language is already an achievement that you should be proud of. It is satisfying to know that you can understand people who speak Dutch and they can understand you when you speak Dutch. Because of this, your confidence will increase because you know that you can do something that not many other people can do. You will stand out among the crowd and you will be known in your group as the person who can speak Dutch.

Chapter 2: Understanding the Dutch Language

Before you learn about the Dutch alphabet, grammar, sentence construction, useful Dutch words and phrases and other basic Dutch lessons, you should first understand the language—how it came about, who speaks it and where it is spoken, among other things. By having a deeper understanding about the language and going beyond the technicalities of the grammar rules, you will find it easier to learn how to speak the language.

Development of the Dutch language

Dutch is closely related to English, German and West Frisian and is categorized as a West Germanic language. The origin of Dutch can be traced from the dialect of Low German called Lower Franconian which had German origins. However, modern Dutch has significantly departed from its original Germanic roots.

Today, the modern Dutch language does not use the German umlaut which is an important grammatical marker in the German language and the language also did not shift to the use of High German consonant. Moreover, the language now uses a grammatical case system which is very much different from the original.

However, the Dutch language still retains some characteristics that are similar to its Germanic origins. For instance, Dutch vocabulary is very similar to German vocabulary. The sentence structure (SOV for subordinate clauses and SVO for main clauses) is still the same as the original Dutch language.

Where is Dutch spoken?

You need to know where you are going to use the language that you are planning to study. In case of the Dutch language, it is considered as the national language in certain European countries such as The Netherlands and Belgium. In Belgium, the northern region of the country called Flanders consider Dutch as their official language and many people in Brussels speak the language, although the majority speaks French.

Dutch is also spoken in Suriname and the Dutch Atilles—the former is located in South America while the latter is located in the Caribbean. Many countries in Europe also speak Dutch such as Germany and France. There are also native Dutch speakers in other parts of the world such as the U.S., Canada, New Zealand and Australia because many Dutch people migrated and established their roots in these countries back in the 1950s.

Is Dutch difficult to learn?

Different languages have different levels of difficulty. For the Dutch language, it is considered one of the easiest languages to learn because it uses almost the same letters as the English alphabet. In terms of difficulty, it falls between the level of English and German. English speakers will find it a lot easier to study Dutch than other languages like Japanese or Russian that have their own symbols.

What's confusing about the Dutch language is its use of the two articles *de* and *het*. In English, there is only one article: *the*, while German has three: *der, die,* and *das*. It is confusing to remember when to use these two Dutch articles because you have to memorize the right article for each noun.

Another difficulty that you may encounter when learning Dutch is its sentence structure. Just like German, the Dutch language also positions the verb at the end of the sentence, unlike English where the verb is in the middle. There are also a lot of little words to learn that change the meaning and mood of the sentence such as *eens, even, maar, nog, nou,* and *toch*. By adding or removing one little word in your sentence, the meaning or mood changes significantly.

Similarities of Dutch and English words

You will be surprised that a lot of English words are similar to their Dutch counterparts. Here are a few examples:

- apple – appel
- banana – banaan
- pear – peer
- tomato - tomaat
- blue – blauw
- green – groen
- red – rood

If you take a look at these words, the Dutch words look similar to the English words. You might even think that the Dutch word is just a typo if you do not speak Dutch. There are also some common English words that were derived from the Dutch language such as *cookie* (from the Dutch word *koekje* which means biscuit), *coleslaw* (from the Dutch word *koolsla* which means cabbage salad), and *Santa Claus* (from the Dutch word *Sinterhlaas* or *Sint Nicholaas* which is translated to Saint Nicholas).

Dutch in social situations

You also need to know how you are going to use Dutch in social situations. For example, there are two Dutch translations for the second pronoun 'you'—the more formal *u* and the casual *je* or *jij*. You need to use *u* when talking to people you do not know like servers and shop employees and *je* or *jij* in all other situations. However, in recent times, people start to use the less formal variation even when talking to people they do not know. It is no longer impolite to be addressed with a *je* or *jij* by a server when you go to a restaurant or bar.

When introducing a friend, you have to be careful because you might make the mistake of implying that the person is your girlfriend or your boyfriend when he or she is not. Instead of saying *mijn vriend* (my male friend) or *mijn vriendin* (my female friend), you should say *een vriend/vriendin* (a friend) when introducing a friend and not a girlfriend or boyfriend.

You will also come across confusing words when you go to a Dutch-speaking country. For example, you will see a sign that says *lagere school* which simply means 'primary school'. When you go to a restaurant and see the word *kip,* it does not refer to a kind of fish because it means 'chicken' in Dutch. When you go to a coffee shop or teahouse and come across the word *slagroom,* you should not confuse it with a special room in the shop because it simply means 'whipped cream'.

Chapter 3: Basic Lessons in Dutch Language

As a beginner, you need to study some basic Dutch words and phrases that you will find useful when communicating with Dutch people. You need to study practical Dutch words and phrases first before you delve deeper into more difficult Dutch lessons because this is something that you can use right away, like when you visit a Dutch-speaking country or when you speak to a native Dutch speaker at work.

Aside from basic Dutch words and phrases, you also need to learn about basic grammar lessons that will help construct sentences in Dutch without too much trouble.

The Dutch alphabet

When learning Dutch or any other language for that matter, it is best to start learning the alphabet. Fortunately, the Dutch alphabet is the same as the English alphabet, although the pronunciation is different. Some of the sounds in the Dutch alphabet are not used in English, which makes it a little difficult to learn, although it will be easier as you get used to the different pronunciations. The letters that have the same sounds for both the Dutch and English alphabets are the consonants, b, d, f, h, l, m, n, s, and z. Some of the letters are formed in the same way but they are not aspirated when pronounced in Dutch, such as k, p, and t.

Noun genders

The Dutch language has two noun genders—*de* for common and *het* for neuter. This is easier than the German noun genders that have three, as what has been mentioned in the previous chapters. What makes this difficult is that you have to memorize the gender of the nouns in the Dutch language because it can be difficult to identify gender based on how the word looks.

The *de* words or the common nouns are a combination of the masculine and feminine genders that are no longer being used in the Dutch language. This is the reason why almost two-thirds of the nouns in the Dutch language belong to the *de* category or the common gender.

So instead of memorizing all the nouns, it is easier to just memorize the neuter nouns that only comprise about 1/3 of the Dutch nouns. Since there are only two groups of nouns, it is safe to assume that those words that you have not memorized are common nouns or *de* words.

How are you going to identify neuter words? Infinites that are used as nouns and diminutive nouns are considered neuter nouns. Dutch words that begin with *be-, ge-,* and *ver-* and words that end in *–aat, -isme, -um-,* and *–sel* are most likely neuter. Words that are always neuter are directions, colors and metals to name a few.

Basic words and phrases

You need to learn some basic words and phrases that you can use when communicating in Dutch. These words are important to learn because they will help you get your meaning across even if your grammar or sentence construction is still not good.

Numbers. You need to memorize the numbers in Dutch because you need this when paying for something, counting money, telling time and date and stating an address, to name a few.

- One – Een /ain/
- Two – Twee /tway/
- Three – Drie /dree/
- Four – Vier /veer/
- Five – Vijf /vayf/
- Six – Zes /zehs/
- Seven – Zeven /zay-vuhn/
- Eight – Acht /ahgt/
- Nine – Negen /nay-guhn/
- Ten – Tien /teen/

Months and days. It is also important to know how to say the days and months in Dutch when you need to set an appointment or a schedule.

- January – Januari /jahn-uu-ar-ee/
- February – Februari /fay-bruu-ah-ree/
- March – Maart /mahrt/
- April – April /ah-pril/
- May –Mei /may/
- June – Juni /yuu-nee/
- July – Juli /yuu-lee/
- August – Augustus /ow-ghus-tus/
- September – September /sep-tem-buhr/
- October – Oktober /ock-tow-buhr/
- November – November /no-vem-buhr/
- December – December /day-sem-buhr/

You will notice that some months have the same spelling for both languages. This makes it easier for non-Dutch speakers to study the language. For the days of the week:

- Monday –Maandag /mahn-dahg/
- Tuesday – Dinsdag /dins-dahg/
- Wednesday – Woensdag /woons-dahg/
- Thursday – Donderdag /don-duhr-dahg/
- Friday – Vrijdag /vray-dahg/
- Saturday – Zaterdag /zah-tuhr-dahg/
- Sunday – Zondag /zon-dahg/

The days of the week are more difficult to identify if you do not know how to speak Dutch because the spelling and pronunciation are completely different from English. It is important to memorize these so that you will not get confused with your appointments and schedules.

Useful words. When communicating with Dutch people, you need to know some useful words that you need to use in conversations. This will greatly improve your conversation skills and will make you more comfortable in social situations where you have to speak Dutch.

- Yes – Ja /yah/
- No – Nee /nay/
- Hello - /hal-low/
- Goodbye – Tot ziens /toht seens/
- Left – Links /links/
- Right – Rechts /reghts/
- Straight ahead – Rechtdoor /regh-dore/
- Please – Alstublieft /ahl-stuu-bleeft/
- Thank you (formal) – Dank u well /dahnk-ew-vehl/
- Thank you (informal) – Dank je wel /dahnk-yuh-vehl/
- Help – Help /hehlp/
- Today – Vandaag /vahn-dahg/
- Tomorrow – Morgen /more-ghun/
- Now – Nu /nuu/
- Later – Later /lah-tuhr/

Phrases. You also need to know some useful phrases that will help you navigate easily in social situations.

- How are you? – Hoe maakt u het? (formal) or Hoe gaat het (informal)
- Fine, thank you. – Goed, dank u. (formal) or Goed, dank je. (informal)
- Nice to meet you. – Aangenaam kennis te maken.
- You are welcome. – Graag gedaan.
- Do you speak English? – Spreekt u Engels? (formal) or Spreek je Engels (informal)
- I don't speak Dutch. – Ik spreek geen Nederlands.
- I speak a little Dutch. – Ik spree keen beetje Nederlands.
- I don't understand. – Ik versta het niet.
- Excuse me. – Excuseer me.

Chapter 4: Tips and Techniques to Gain Fluency

After learning about the basic Dutch lessons, you now need to find out some tips and techniques for gaining fluency. Gaining fluency in speaking Dutch leads to better understanding. It allows you to communicate with Dutch-speaking people no matter what the topic or situation without feeling awkward about it. To improve your fluency in speaking Dutch, here are some things that you need to do.

Gather useful resources for learning Dutch

There are so many resources that can help you learn how to speak Dutch. You can go to your local library and borrow books about learning how to speak Dutch. This is ideal for people who live near the library. The good thing about borrowing books from the library is that you do not need to pay for anything as long as you return the books on time. If there is no local library in your immediate vicinity, you can always go to a bookstore and buy a book about learning Dutch. It is important to buy yourself a good bilingual dictionary that will be useful when studying Dutch or traveling in Dutch-speaking countries and you need to translate English words to Dutch words and vice versa.

Aside from books, you can also go to websites that teach Dutch for free. You can find different learning materials from these websites such as workbooks, online dictionaries, audio books and videos.

Hire a Dutch tutor or enroll in a Dutch course

You can hire an online Dutch tutor where you can communicate via chat or online calls or you can hire a Dutch native who live in your area to teach you how to speak Dutch. You can also enroll in Dutch classes online or in your community. Some people find it difficult to study a language by themselves and need the help and guidance of a teacher. Some people also prefer learning a language from a real person than from a book because they can observe nuances in the language that they cannot observe by simply reading a book. Some people also believe that they will learn a lot more about the Dutch culture when talking to a native Dutch speaker.

Of course, you need to pay the private tutor or the registration fee so be sure to set aside a budget for this.

Enhance your listening skills

It is important to enhance your listening skills because this can help you communicate better using Dutch. To do this, you should listen to as much Dutch as possible using audio books or by watching Dutch tutorials in YouTube. If you visit a Dutch speaking country, you should listen carefully to the people around you so that you will hear how the words really sound and how the language flows when used in actual conversations.

Speak Dutch as often as you can

The best way to gain fluency is to speak Dutch as often as you can. You already know the saying practice makes perfect and how it applies to learning new things such as learning how to speak a foreign language. You will commit a lot of mistakes at first but it is normal because you are just starting to learn the language. Do not get discouraged if you find it difficult at first because it takes a lot more than a few days or even weeks to be fluent in a foreign language.

To practice Dutch at home, you should consider replying in English first then translating your reply in Dutch afterwards. Of course, it is important to let your family know that you are learning how to speak Dutch so that they will not think that you have been abducted by aliens and is now speaking an alien language. It would be really helpful if a family member knows how to speak Dutch or is also studying it like you.

When talking to a native Dutch speaker, you should use Dutch instead of English no matter how much you are struggling and even if the person responded in English. This will practice your ability to communicate in Dutch with someone who speaks it naturally.

You can also change the language settings in your phone, computer or social media accounts from English to Dutch. This will help you practice Dutch in a more technical setting.

Visit Dutch-speaking countries

If you have the money and time, you should consider visiting a Dutch-speaking country where you can listen to natives speak Dutch and practice your speaking skills with a native speaker. You can visit The Netherlands, Belgium, Suriname, and Dutch Atilles if you want to immerse yourself in the language. Visiting Dutch-speaking countries will also help you learn more about the culture and the people who speak the language.

You will see how they interact with one another in different social circumstances using the Dutch language. You can stay there for a few days or even weeks on vacation or you can enroll in a cultural exchange program for foreigners who want to study Dutch and other courses abroad.

Keep your mind open

When learning a foreign language, you need to keep an open mind because you will find a lot of differences between the language that you are learning and the language that you were born and raised with. You are also learning a new culture which is very much different from your own. Do not let your initial impressions and expectations and cultural stereotypes get in the way of understanding the Dutch language and culture.

Chapter 5: Common Mistakes to Avoid

When studying the Dutch language, it is important to know the common mistakes that you need to avoid to ensure that the whole process becomes smooth sailing. Some people think that the language is too difficult to learn or that there is something wrong with their ability to learn a language because they cannot see any progress. You should not be too hard on yourself or on the language that you are learning because it might be because your whole approach is completely wrong.

Below is a list of some of the most common mistakes that you need to avoid when learning the Dutch language.

Thinking that memorizing Dutch words and phrases is enough

Some people think that all they need to do to learn a language is to know the translation of words from English to Dutch. They think that learning how to communicate using the language will just follow once they know which keywords to use. For these people, memorization is enough because you will soon get the hang of it as you listen to and immerse in the language.

Memorization is important in learning a new language but it is not enough. There is more to language than simply memorizing the words and phrases. For example, you need to know the proper order of words in a sentence and you also need to understand how to say things politely. You should also know that certain words could have more than one meaning and it is important that you are able to identify which meaning is being referred to. There are some words that change in meaning depending on the context so be sure to learn the Dutch language beyond memorizing words and phrases.

Believing that Dutch immersion is the fastest way to learn

Although staying or living in a Dutch-speaking country and communicating with Dutch people on a daily basis is extremely helpful in learning the language, you still need to do it properly. For instance, beginners should not instantly expose themselves to too much Dutch language because they might feel overwhelmed and confused. Too much information can make your brain switch off which will make it even more difficult for you to learn. What you can do is to prepare yourself first by learning some basic Dutch language lessons before you go out to the real world and expose yourself to the language in real-life situations. If you do not have the basic knowledge of Dutch vocabulary, grammar and syntax, you will not be able to handle conversations in Dutch.

Learning Dutch after work

Many people who want to learn Dutch are busy with their regular jobs. This is why they can only take Dutch lessons at night after work. However, this may not be as effective as you think because you are already tired from work and your brain may no longer be receptive. You might feel sleepy while listening to your Dutch tutor and it will just be a waste of time not to mention money because your brain is not absorbing anything. What you can do instead is to set a day every weekend when you can learn Dutch, like every Saturday or Sunday when your mind and body are not too tired from work.

Treating it as homework

Many people make the mistake of treating the whole process of learning a new language as homework, unlike learning a musical instrument or a new sport. This is probably because they associate it with studying English, French, or Spanish at school. If you treat it as a homework, it takes the fun out of learning a new language because your mind perceives it as a chore or as something that has to be done. To prevent yourself from getting bored, you should see learning Dutch as an enjoyable process that allows you to learn more about a different culture. Do not focus too much on the boring aspect of learning such as taking a quiz, grammar drills, memorization and reading a textbook but concentrate on the more interesting things about the language.

To make it enjoyable, you can do activities involving the Dutch language such as watching Dutch movies, listening to Dutch music, visiting Dutch-speaking countries and going to Dutch museums.

Using only a single method

Learning a new language requires diversity in terms of the methods and strategies that you need to use. If you are stuck in the same textbook for months, maybe it is time for you to try other methods of learning Dutch such as listening to audio books, practicing speaking exercises, reading Dutch books and immersing in Dutch culture. Language is not something that you can learn from one textbook. It requires you to experience the language rather than simply learning everything in your tutorial class.

Diversifying your methods will also make your lessons more enjoyable because you have something new to look forward to as you are learning how communicate using the Dutch language.

Conclusion

Thank you again for purchasing this book!

I hope this book was able to help you to take the first few steps in learning to speak Greek.

The next step is to persist in becoming an expert.

Finally, if you enjoyed this book, please take the time to share your thoughts and post a review on Amazon. We do our best to reach out to readers and provide the best value we can. Your positive review will help us achieve that. It'd be greatly appreciated!

Thank you and good luck!

Check Out My Other Books

Below you'll find some of my other popular books that are popular on Amazon and Kindle as well. Simply click on the links below to check them out. Alternatively, you can visit my author page on Amazon to see other work done by me.

The Best of England For Tourists

http://amzn.to/1rv7RVZ

The Best of Brazil For Tourists

http://amzn.to/1sCoSdT

The Best of Beautiful Greece For Tourists

http://amzn.to/1u9Xclw

The Best of Spain For Tourists

http://amzn.to/1zHGGII

The Best of Beautiful Germany For Tourists

http://amzn.to/V4SoiT

The Best of Beautiful France For Tourists

http://amzn.to/1yD7yal

The Best of Beautiful Netherlands For Tourists

http://amzn.to/1oU2hKF

The Best of Italy For Tourists

http://amzn.to/1kNIqYm

Portuguese for Beginners

http://amzn.to/1qgRyKH

Greek for Beginners

http://amzn.to/1u385SO

German for Beginners

http://amzn.to/Y3JxOV

French for Beginners

http://amzn.to/1CgsxVc

Dutch for Beginners

http://amzn.to/1pZhdb3

English for Beginners

http://amzn.to/1qZbmCz

Italian for Beginners

http://amzn.to/1pxjRFL

Spanish for Beginners

http://amzn.to/1lDoJFr

Travel Box Set #1 The Best of Brazil For Tourists & Portuguese for Beginners

http://amzn.to/W0FSzA

Travel Box Set #2 The Best of England For Tourists & English for Beginners

http://amzn.to/Y3M2kv

Travel Box Set #3 The Best of Beautiful France For Tourists & French for Beginners

http://amzn.to/1Cgv0gX

Travel Box Set #4 The Best of Beautiful Germany For Tourists & German for Beginners

http://amzn.to/1qgUF5y

Travel Box Set #5 The Best of Beautiful Greece For Tourists & Greek for Beginners

http://amzn.to/1phepk9

If the links do not work, for whatever reason, you can simply search for these titles on the Amazon website to find them

Printed in Germany
by Amazon Distribution
GmbH, Leipzig